# The Book Of Poetry

By Kaleel John

GW00468322

Labworks Publishing Inc.
2022 Copyright
All Rights Reserved

# A Black Man's Poetic Journey Through Love, Pleasure and Pain

# Start Here

Historically, the Black Book has meant different things to different people. Generally speaking, it was a book of secrets.

As you unpack my "Secrets" while walking down the streets of my mind, you will see glimpses of my choices, hopes, dreams, fears and anxieties.

My hope is that you will find a gem that you could use in your own life or inspire you creatively. I challenge you to find new ways to express yourself other than those you are accustomed to.

Embark on this journey into my historical and present-day mind, get your fix for my words rhythmically sown together - My Poetry.

# CONTENTS

# CONTENTS

# GENESIS

# Liberation

I've been evading my freedom of expression
This pen, this pad, my breath
To bleed my soul as ink through this pen

LIBERATION

That helps me escape death
I've internally wept
And my emotions, they crept
Onto the canvas or landscape of this paper
To be expressed

FULLY

Nothing kept or left inside
Nothing kept to hide
As I breathe with the ink of my soul on this pad
To inhale and exhale become easy
Writing has now become my ecstasy
To bleed my soul as ink through this pen to my pad
PURE ENERGY

Liberation

# Introspection

I want to say sorry
Sorry to all the women that I've loved and lost
or never loved at all.
To the ones I've hurt or who hurt me
Broken to the unimaginability
I'm older now, much wiser
but it came at a cost
A trail of broken hearts
a cause for pause
A reflective light too late I'd sight
Misery measured weigh my plight
Hard to see, blessed now cloaks me night
Internal war beyond the see
powerful enough to destroy me
Without you, there'd be no me
I hope you're well is well
Cracks in glass
cannot tell
Pray for me
reverse the spell

# Lucid Moments #1

I'm at a crossroads right now to either be a loser for the rest of my life or get an education and become a professional.

I don't know why I have wasted so much time doing things and not being qualified in those areas.

Babblings of a high school dropout

-Some time in 2011

# Stats and Stereotypes

Every woman I've ever been with I have beaten.
They act up?
I lay the smackdown.
I have 10 kids with 9 different women.
I have been to jail over 7 times before my 21st birthday.
I get into fights on a regular basis.
I walk around with a chip on my shoulder, ready to blame everyone for my problems.
I will beat you, I will rob you, and yes, I steal.
Why do you look so alarmed? Aren't those the same thoughts going through your mind right now?
You were saying, "I bet he's been to jail."
Is it hard to tell?
It's easier to lump me in and fear me than spend time getting to know me.

# Stats and Stereotypes...

They say that it is more likely for a Black Man to go to jail
than go to college. My brothers, my sisters, I will not be that
"Stereo's" type, and I will not be that image that might be
coursing through some of your minds.
He is...
Caressing corners
Handing out packets of absolute bliss...
Takes away lives with a kiss of connected hands
It's hard to stand up in this cold world as a real man...
Hey! Black Man
Real men don't cry
back down
get disrespected
or take BACKCHAT from NO woman
These statements are open doors for emotionally unstable
men - men with no outlets for the welling up of stubborn
pride; they can't bend
Ridged
May break
Got to escape the odds
I escaped the odds
Thus far

# My Brand of Man

I am not a stereotype
Even if I fit it before
I no longer fit it
I am bigger and louder than the "Stereo's" type
So I have the ammunition to fight
The ideals of the day and the stigma of the past
I am bigger than the "Stereo's" sound
Life's popular sound and what it's saying about this generation
Of what it says to be Black
I rebel against the "Stereo's" type
I will not leave my children fatherless
I will work a job till I can own my business
The white man is NOT my problem
I am my worst enemy and one of my greatest allies
Without MY cooperation I will die
I will not beat my women
I will cherish her as life itself
My sister, my love, my friend
I will not become part of an inmate population
It is not a part of my innate nature
I am louder than the popular message
That old sound
That Ancient story that the "Stereo" plays about me
I am a giant in this world, larger than life
I'll leave my mark and it will be large
They will know me, they will know my name
This is not a claim to fame but a shout for change
Not for the world but for my name
I start today by playing a new sound through the stereo
Hopefully, it's loud enough for the world to know

# My Brand of Man - Con't

That whom I want to be is how they see me be
And with that, no discrepancy, only synergy
I am a businessman
I am a writer
I am a producer of television and film
I invest in real estate
I put deals together
People trust me
I am trustworthy
I am creative
I am focused
I know what I want
My image is now out there
It plays through the stereo and it is loud
No longer hearing the "stereos type"
MY image is loud
It is proud
My Brand of Man

# Midnight Madness

It's been a very long time since I've been inspired to write something of
substance; It's been harder to find
Is this all real?
Has reality set in?
Is this truly where I am?
Illusions used to be a regular thing, an ugly game that I couldn't win

Now it's like reality wants to hold on to me
Holding grasp of me
Won't let go of me
But I can't seem to tell which is which
Has my inspiration left me?
That constant challenge of my mind and body, has it left me?

Was it in a woman or just in my mind?
Or did my experience elude this test of time?
I want it back; I want it all back!
My inspiration was like my child. It motivated me to work hard, push
forward for better days, and seek positivity throughout the foggy streets of
my life's night
This is my truth; I cannot breathe with no relief
I've lost my seed

Overwhelmed is an understatement
Punishment, is it?
Well, I rebel against the drudgery of my life's irony
Lost a few mental petals through it all
Steam whistle, there goes the kettle
enough to wake me up
It is burning, why does it scald?
But I already know the answers to it all
Midnight Madness

# VOYAGE

16

# Alone at sea

"A soft touch, a gentle caress
Is all I need
**Denial is Murder**
Slow is Murder"

I don't know you that well, but somehow I am intrigued by you.
Your smile drawing me closer, I try to see if ill hear a word
That might express the smile that I see, not knowing its your
silence that's keeping me

(DRAWN)

What a bittersweet, not knowing what's next, EXCITEMENT!
But not seeing the physical embodiment of what you express in
spoken word to me

(MURDER)

To everything that I hold dear to me, to everything I try to
understand to see
To everything I aspire to be, to holding you close to me
To everything that you express to be or the feelings you can't
portray to me

It's Murder, Slow Murder

You say you do but you don't. You wish you did but you won't
( A slow Murder)
Your feelings are trapped inside, the ones you try hard to hide, it's
all Murder....
To Me
To everything that is trying to grow, I just thought I'd let you
know....Slow Murder

# Alone at sea...

It's like...I feel I'm paddling this boat by myself; without any help
But yet I can't see me rowing with no one else... A Slow Murder

In a sea with no end in sight and I'm rowing with all my might...
Slow Murder

Are you gonna help me paddle now?
I promise, we would get somewhere, somehow
Not knowing quite how to get there, but knowing we will arrive
With a little blood sweat and tears, we'll make it
Without you, it's Murder

Sometimes don't feel to pick up the phone, cause I feel like I am all
alone.

I feel that maybe if I get lost, you'll come to find me
If you really wanted to, you'll search for me
When you're ready you'll come for me

It's a Slow Murder

If you'll only show me some interest I'd be fine
But for now, what should I do?
Should I let you go and say, if it is meant to be, it will be?
Letting go and hoping that you'll come for me?
Or hold on knowing that it's supposed to be...
It's a Slow Murder

# The Path Of A Broken Man

Blessed days unique realizations
Sitting while contemplating
Certain things are revealed not to be good
While other things seem to be allies
I don't cry; I man up; I stand up to face each fight
Part of being a man
No longer a man-child
Developing growing learning reaching
Still, a ways off from where I want to be
Living my life is what I intend
Story unfolding, I want to see the end
Carefully selecting choices
Neglecting voices
Boasting
Coercing
Splendid courses

# The taming
# of the untameable heart

Dear the one I could not help but to love, knowing you were sent
from above. Descend on me like a dove with all of your love. Don't
hold back.


Now what kind of man would I be
If I stopped writing to you with my heart on paper
Just because things seemed a little more stable
Or that I would not take the time to spend to chase
you
Who would I be?

> I would be a lost man, a man without vision
> An unstable man that lacked precision
> A man that was burdened with so much on his chest
> Looking for someone just to relieve his stress
> Cause his life would truly be a mess
> BE BLESSED

Cause the remedy I found in you
And I'ma treat you like a Queen, and you know its true
I'd take my heart out of my body to lay my heart on your
chest
It's nothing for me to give my heart to my other half
I am just giving it over to my other self
Another image of me, that without her being, I would
never be

If I die, I'll still live on in you, cause the heart that I have will forever beat for you

My heart has found a new home with flesh of my flesh and bone of my bone

I am going to love you till there is no breath left

We're the same except, for the breath that is in us

And the womb in you that would one day bear our fruit and that's the truth

So if I'm not here, I'm still here, living on in all of you.

Take care of my heart

# Pain...Unfiltered

My seeds were dashed
My dreams have crashed
Upon the rocks ashore
My teeth they gnashed
As my heart is smashed
And broken at its core

The visions fade
In comes pain
To disrupt my very soul
Insanity lingers
The pointing of fingers
Is like the pulling of triggers
But words as bullets enter inside

Internal damage
My heart is in anguish
My mind state is ravished

Love escaped me

# Pain...Unfiltered...

I've been penetrated by distorted images of what really was
By vile words that cut so deep
But there are no external puncture wounds to see

The only evidence of internal damage was the expression of pain &
confusion
Because I lived an illusion

Thought it was love I was receiving
But it was lies that were deceiving
Her words I was believing
Cause she was my girl

She said that she loved me
And that she would not leave
Ride or die she said

ALL LIES!!!

Even to the point where we said our goodbyes

Signal the Doves to Cry

# Real Pain

My heart was on paper
ripped to shreds
No regard
by me
Broke the glass
glasshouse
shards upon the floor
Can't breathe
no air
Anxiety's grips are cold
Its noose on tight
Hangman
No real control
Darkness seeps through the cracks of the
void of light alleyways
Memories
Lost for words
Core in overload
I was brought to tears
But tears did not have mercy upon my eyes
It left them red and bruised
Heart is bursting
Thirsting
for a pain to which it cannot subscribe

# CONFESS

26

You are cherished
These words flow through me
Poetry's Flowetry
Confidentiality's openness
Hoping no line will be revoked from this
Rhyme and reason
As I'm Choked up on these words
They must come out
Loud and clear
But as not to shout
You're my Everything's everything
You are to me everything
You are cherished
Your heart
Your mind
Your soul
Your essence
is cherished
You are the sweetest Blessing
Gift unwrapped
Everything wrong I've done, I take back
In fact
I just want to forget about all of that
And take time to take a part every layer of your wrapping
Just to hold the gift on its inside
My intent I cannot hide
You are Beauty's gift
Beauty could not live if it could not
be expressed through you
Day by day, I see it too
You are cherished

Cherished

# Everything

Everything in me
When I die will be out
I'm not talking about the bile, the waste and all the things the body rejects
I'm talking bout my dreams, my visions,
every poem, lyrically written, lyrically spoken will come out
Every film in me deposited by the Most-High and those given by the
creativity he has given me
I want to be empty
Every book written
Not to bless me but to bless the world
Everything

# Them Words

Words?
I got them
I got them all to say the things I want them to say
But what are words that can't portray what you need to hear me say?

They become useless utterances
vain babbling for birds to catch in the wind
If I can send a clear message it would be that I still...
love you
And though it may not matter and though you may not care
I still do
If I have thoughts of you every waking moment of every second of
the day
And I feen for you like I lost something, like I missed a fix, like my
other half... Missed

This internal battle mixed with pride kept me from pursuing you
My own Selfishness writes this letter to a person I don't deserve
cause as I lost you, I lost myself indefinitely
So I live through these Poems and I live through my dreams
where we commune together in perfect peace
If my words mattered I would apologize to you and say I am sorry
Throwing away all pride, any hope of redemption or any hope of
saving face, all tossed out the window to the point of disgrace.
It all doesn't matter, does it?
I mean it's been too long, I mean you've probably moved on
most likely in love
Would it be enough to repair the damage to my soul?
My words
useless words

# What's left?!

Should I burn all these pictures?
Along with our memories
So many things frozen in time
to remind us of what was
Should we burn like paper
on the darkroom floor?

High fever but cold to the touch
My mind hurts
Cause what runs through it
Is bathing in heat
Torched by the opposite
of what ignited us to love

It catches fast
from the pictures
to the memories
to our hearts

Engulfed

Cold sweats trying to relieve us of the smoke
caught in our lungs
can't breathe no more
Clouding our eyes, we can't see
not in front of us
not you and me
We are so close
but yet, so far
the smoke becomes our walls

# What's left?! Cont...

These pictures

only captured the good times
the bad ones only etched in memories
What led us here? I ask myself
If we unite once more, will things be the same
Should I fight for it?
Or let it go in flames

In the end
All I have
All that is left
are pictures

# Everyday Usual

Every day I grow closer and closer to you
Like sun rays crashing and peeking through your windowpane
Just to clothe you with my warmth is what I live for

Every dark cloud I will remove with the beams of my heart
with our love that crossed mountains to break through the dark
the love that conquered death that tried to rip us apart

You are exactly whom I envisioned you to be
and who you are to become, I can clearly see
I only captured a fraction of what you really could be

It's crazy, see
It's you and me
On the battlefront of the future
As we fight our past
Clothed in honour
Crack the hourglass
Time matters no more
For the thing we've raced against to attain
we now have
and more
GOD IS GOOD

# CHAINED

34

# UNCHAINED

My unexpected love
You stole my heart
I gave It up
Not an easy battle t'was
Beauty for ashes
yes It was
You still have It all
It holds me where I am
take this pain away
No
here I am to stay
wipe these fears away
Mould this heart of clay
I'm missing
cause your missing
Your cooking and your kissing
Your hips kissed
Kissed lips
To miss positions
missed each other
swift to grip and sip another
locked to clip a wrist
uncovered
Bound but free Unchain each other

# Pre Murder

I feel your cold hard hands
wrapped around my throat
like a noose
Gripping
Tighter and tighter
Tighter as I try to
Try to pull away
Tighter
as I reach for life
Tighter
As I try to live
Cradled in fetal position
Cribbed in non-motion
Knees to chest
Arms to rest
Shivers
Heart too stressed
Blood leaves limbs
I try to open my eyes
To see what's left
Beyond this
This feeling of hopelessness
Helpless
Because you're trying to take my life
Anxiety
Crippled
Out of sight
You took the day
I pray with peace
I take the night

# Realizations

I never thought I would ever feel this way about you.
I'm finding that the love I have for you has gone through the fire and still
remains true.

It's like every other woman fails in comparison to you.
Their beauty is not enough to draw me any longer; your inner beauty
outshines them all, no longer looking for something to be wrong.

Now only basking in what's right, what's pure, what's true.

It's like no matter how pissed off I get at you, our love draws me back to
you. You now have become my inspiration for love
it seems like every hour of the day that's all I'm thinking of.
It nudges and pushes me closer, I cannot get enough of you.

Your "*Womaninity*" covers me and strengthens to my core to be... Man.

It's more than I ever asked for, I'm looking at the impossible as possible
I understand now, that to love you with every inch of me, to the point of
the filling of you, is the purest way to unite our truth. The only way I can
love myself is to truly love you.

Realizations.

# Lucid Moments #2

## Vapour

We are but a vapour
A glimmer of light
A glimmer of hope to be fulfilled
Sent to shine through the darkness
Shine in the night
Like shooting stars
For a fleeting moment
But a moment in time

## Closure

I used to want closure but then I realized closure was an illusion designed to keep one tied to their past. It does not exist. You cannot just talk about something and expect everything you feel to go away. You have to make a conscious decision not to allow what you feel to keep you in the same place.

# They Say

They say that everything is possible
But I know that is not possible
Like getting back with you is impossible
I mean like digging yourself out of a hole
Like, ain't that the real goal?
Scream to the depths of your soul
My punishment alone

I know that it's all so impossible
What if the impossible were possible
Would it be that improbable
I would be that much more unstoppable

Looking into your eyes is impossible
But if the improbable were probable
I would be weak in the knees from telling you I love you
and that I'm missing you

Hope is nothing but a ruse that forces us to choose the probable and the
possible and to forget the impossible without it leaving any clues

I know that touching you is impossible
like not at all possible
So if that "possible" is not probable even though I wish it were possible
The dream is now corruptible
Wishing, a dying fad.

# Just a Shell of a Man

Just a shell of a man
Can't stand
Not what I used to be
No jokes
All laughter blown away
Things I used to care for fade away
And it seems as if dreams are my only release
Fairytales to find peace
Peace hides behind my insanity

# REALITY

42

# Life

You take my breath away
Then give it all back.
an influx of air that can't be matched
Can be too much but gives me life
I know the fragility of your heart
and you know that of mine
They are enclosed in our embrace
protected in our love.
Caged

# Suffer

So you wanna see me suffer
Well now I'm suffering
to my very soul
Corrosion now settles in
So bet you think that's nice
you want no recovering
Broken to my core
Insane sorta tumbles in
Says a lot about you
No mercy no forgiveness

# True things

Knives from our mouths
cut deep,
deeper than real knives
Kills our souls
Takes our lives
We become living dead

# Truth's Experience

Seems like my life is like a soap opera
A city of dreams
Built on lust and lies
And hopes that scream
When peace is shattered
And beauty seethes
An intense love so strong
I could hardly breathe
Crushed beyond measure
Hearts beat subsides
No tears all fears
Now tongue-tied
Blinded eyes only see what the mind shows it to be
And if the mind is corrupt
Its visions are hopeless
Crossed eyed
Lost focus

# Reality's Show

I'm not blind
I know what it is now
No longer in denial
I got it
I feel now

I already understand the language of silence
It speaks clear
More than the words you let me hear

It's kool, I understand
Things sometimes happen this way
No point in changing it
It was meant to be this way

Realest things that ever happened
Smoke, puff, it's gone
No more pretend
No crying
This was ceased up from the beginning and straight to the end
Forced what should not have been
Now living consequences

Things could not have changed without effort
The way you looked
You wanted silence
And to straight overlook
Or when you were ready to maybe take a look
you'd expect things to be ok

# Reality's Show

But we're not robots
We are human beings
We feel and we see
I Just felt you wouldn't be satisfied until I bleed

Friends are gone, who were they?
Two-Faced
Double Masks
are now see through
I trust no one but myself
Your treachery
Keep to yourself
I'm Tired, you've won
I'm done

No longer taking it
Can't breathe can't see
no longer faking it
See you on the other side
of what began
No turning back

# Back To You

Back to you
I give it all back
and not a second too soon
I give it all back to you

I give you back the guilt
That was given to me through our situation
The months of pacing back and forth
Waiting for my mind to be made up
I give back
Not being able to get you out of my mind
Running Chasing memories that fly

I give it all back to you
Everything that once was
That now isn't
All to you
No longer holding on to shadows of our diluted past

I do not want this regret that you gave to me subliminally
Telling me one day I will know what it is to lose you
Take all this pain of the thought of me hurting you and running
away with my heart
The truths I told that are now lies that have torn us apart
Take away this love I still got for you
That haunts my every intention to be a better man
Take the gaze you used to give me but still give me in my mind
A look of love I have now seen a thousand times
Like pictures through a movie projector, frozen pictures become alive
Telling all the stories of a lost love and a lost time

# Back To You...Con't

Take it all back
Like sharpened poison arrows
They dig deeper with every waking moment I'm alive
Like they were shot with purpose to be released in time
Time is the syringe that releases the poison inside
Cleverly put
A part of me died
Ever since that day been trying to revive

I give it all back to you
The many "you were wrong" and "I was right"
The turning away without a fight
Purposeless innuendos petty insinuations
Take back the bigger picture that now plays on widescreen
Because I the conductor didn't like when things didn't go my steam
All back to you

# Blurred Lines

I know you want your space and all of that; I mean, do I have a choice?
Your wish is my command, so I silence my voice and step back a little bit to give you room to breathe, but things aren't what they seem

Now I find myself regretting but in the process; I have been taught some valuable lessons

If you are close with someone and y'all are vibing, don't cross blurred lines; you got to watch the timing
Cross them only if you are absolutely sure you know what you want because you can end up losing a friend when a friendship is all you got; you know when it means so much?

It meant something to me, that is why I write you
What now? Now you take your space, and we have lost our rapport

Would we ever get back the friendship we once had, with the dream of business domination or is it too late for that? I don't know, but these are things that are on my mind

It could very well be that we will turn out just fine, taking it one day at a time.
We have now become a piece of the song or just one of Musiq's lines

I really hate what has happened with us, honestly, this is what I wanted to avoid. This is so crazy or just Half Crazy that we let passion cloud our decision-making, losing the most valuable part of what was growing or trying to grow.

Our friendship.

# Forbidden

Lovers deep, lovers creep
Two together our lovers sleep
Unbeknownst our lovers be
Under siege our lovers keep
Secrets toil so that they won't seep
through the cracks of forbidden street
Tarnished are the memories of lovers' old
Lovers broke certain lines of unspoken code
Point of no return
Indwelling thoughts dwell
Wrapped and entangled from a spell
From the stories we weave
To the lies that deceive
Caught!!!
Now
what a relief
No more cries from the deep
Or walking on forbidden street

# Peace

Peace is as Peace does
But not without one's sacrifice
Not without the shedding of light
Not blood
To a generation full of fight
Not to alone take a piece of Peace
But Peace as a whole, to all of humanity
For restoration, abandoning sleepless nights
The resolution is a revolution
Restitution to the cleansing of our mind's sight
No more clouding to the cloaking cloak of dark's night
But we see because of the light
Illuminating peace to sight
In the end, Peace was right
Peace + Love = Sight
Give Peace

# MENTAL

You blew my mind
all over the kitchen table
fragments of pieces
pieces of fragments
of who I thought I was
Broken
to the unrecognizable
Undisguised
chapters
Soaked up with the essence of life
crying out from the cracks
Brokeness
Strands of wood
to openness
thoughts scattered
hopelessness
But now you got the big picture
All the cards on the table
Pieces of me
In your hands
You captured
Pieces of me
I cease to be
The same things change

# FITS OF USUAL

Broken glass
A broken phone
Quick to dash within a flash
Be gone
Center stage
Full off rage
It's on
Inoculated nocturnal
Waited patient
Vacated
Lights of night chasing
Red and blue leak through
Misplaced it
Seems the bloody truth
Erased
It's lies
I'm telling you
No escaping

# EQUIPOSE

54

# Prejudice Paradise

Why do I feel this way
Feel like a villain
Vilified and I ain't one
Walking down the street with eyes to floor
crossing the street
just so that you can feel comfortable enough to come out  of your car
Why does your prejudice affect me so?
to where I play prejudice all on my own
In my mind
Trying to atone
Caught up by lies
Cut off all ties to reality, a victim of precrime
Have you ever owned prejudice?
Or was that mine?
Playing over and over again in my mind
trying to pigeonhole you to something you're not guilty of
maybe...
I'm looking at me through your eyes but they're not your eyes
Looking through the smudged lens of my experience, my demise
I see you as your predecessors
Random people I see in the streets that display prejudice to me
I in turn do it to you
It's how I survive
It's how I stay safe
Guess it's the same for you
Our pre-judge dice
We roll
Chances toll
Deluded souls

Warmest feelings
Closest closeness
Open hopeless
Broken dreams are mended
Mended dreams been broken
Home
Where your heart is
Where is your heart?
Heart where are you?
Lost in situations
Can't find you here
If I can't find my heart, I can't find my home
Alone
Remember
Those
Sweet smells of seasoning that bring all around
Often the catalyst for happiness or brokenness
Holidays, are you home? Is she there? Can you find her?
Heart!
Don't run away
I need you to connect
Connect with the rhythm
Rhythm of your beat
Rhythm of family
Rhythm of...
Home
Don't flatline
Don't turn to stone
Home can hurt but home is home
Home is where the heart is
If heart can't find home
Heart can be home
Not hopeless
Welcome

Thriving in discord
Is the feel I feel
Fixing
not options
Sadistic
To live on the edge
To push to the end
Watch it bend
To might break
What is this?
What is this place?
What is this feeling?
Me
Inside me

Past breaking through
Unknown feared
In twinned in there
Not a care
Sirens calling
Heartstrings pulled
Deceptive
Coercing
Noise Some Bull

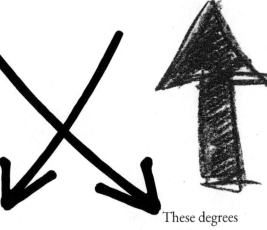

Is this really me
Or the voice in me
Manipulating situations pacing
Blatant places
Might catch cases
Face it
Faceless
Results end
Tasteless

These degrees
Infernos deep
Close to hell
Voices keep
Clear call
So distinct
Corpses shell
Hollow stares
Not in there

FLIPPED

# THE EXPRESS

This breath suffered death
At the hand of neglect
The hand of fear
Caught in this snare
Darks darkest depths
Absent of light
Void of hope
Closed doors hold secrets
Go ignored
Silent cries engulfed
Freedoms voice
In padded cells blackened
How to rebel
How to excel
Victories shout snuffed out
Masked with sin
Bask in doubt
Cells within
Path of the proud
Find the keys to this crypt
Uncertainty
Bring light to life to break chains this plight Of ancients spell
Without it, With it, I will dwell
Rebel
Against a chain of feelings chains
Hard against the grain
To breathe again
Live again
Victory cries, creativity breathes out
Expressions
Relate
Expression emancipates

# Face to Face

I love you and I don't even know you
I smell you like yesterday's dew
Today
Is here, but you're not here
Yet this is the age of anticipation
Waiting with elation
For you to breach this world
I miss you
All of you
The way you are
Or how I imagine you
To be
Or
Not to be
Is not a question
But retaliation
Against the might not be's
Against thoughts without you
Even though I don't have you
Physically
Without you
I've dreamt about you
Countless times
Big smiles
Cute laughs
In my mind
You abide
In my heart
You hide
I can't wait to see your faces
All sides
Both sides
With God's grace and his pace
Face to face

# Catch It

Here we go again
Chasing after the wind
Is it possible?
Is it attainable?
What if I told you it is
Would you believe me?
What if I told you, you could hold it
For but a brief moment
But for that moment you own it
The wind that so graciously goes where it wants to
Been halfway across the world and back
It's yours for but a moment
You know what?
I'll tell you
But it would take one minute of your time
and it would alter your state of mind
All you have to do to catch it is
Breathe In....

# ELEGY

62

# Lost Ones

GONE
Nowhere to be found
Lost forever off the face of the earth
Cold frigid shivers
Black dark nights
Lifeless hearts bring pain to those around
As they wait in agony for mother justice and her
Sometimes slow hand
If only father God could intervene by pointing them out
So that justice may be satisfied
And so that she could then give birth to answers
Or prick the hearts of those who committed the crimes
To come forward, one or all at a time
Or face karma's blow and God's judgment in the afterlife
Let them not sleep or have rest
Let them see the faces
Of the ones they erased to waste away
with every breath, they take till their mind and emotion
Become their prison
Till they can no longer stand living

# Lost Ones...

Bodies cry blood
Blood dries
Tears wet
Soul gone
heart swept
Up in the violence
Screams silenced
The earth is a little lighter now
Released are some bodies from the scale of the world
Only memories take their place
Skewed images instead of their beautiful faces
Left their home innocent
Not expecting to become a murder case
Files on a rectangular desk
They wiped off the smile of an innocent child
Life stops
Words said
But they're not enough to fill the void here
Denial comes
She screams loudly
What are we gonna do without you?
Gone

# Lucid Moments #3

Every single day you show me how to treat you
You teach me how to see you
What you do or don't do to me
You say with your action and inaction what you want me to say
or do
or don't say
or don't do
every single day.
Your favourite student
Class in session

Keep going
keep glowing
Still stay the same
refuse to change
I'm learning
Keep preaching, you old royalty
Spite befalls you
pride becomes you
You have been dethroned.
Reclaim your glory once more.

# MAYBE

Maybe I'm not deserving of whatever this is
Asking self the question
Was I really prepared
For all of this emotion and all it entailed?
It clouds judgement to the point it could fail
Where oft should be clarity corruption walks in
Easily angered hot-tempered aren't characteristics of love
Blinded by rage set afire by loves....evil cousin jealousy
Used tools of visualization, seduced to peril
Dismissal of issues produces strangers who are commonly known
Playing tag, broken telephone
Provoked to anger apologies accepted
Hopefully past won't be used as weapons to re-inflict the pain in our
present

# Voice Of The Broken

Are you there?
Have you gone away?
Have you left me alone?
Do you even care?
Broken hearts are left as tokens to constantly remind us of fruitless
seeds, that we wish were but were not to be.

June 12 2006 2:23 PM

# Guard Your Heart

Whoever has your heart has the power to control and destroy you, or to build you up to renew you. You never make someone your world, you make them a part of your world. That way if they leave they don't take your world with them.

8-Feb-2007 6:35 PM

# Truth

Truth is what the Truth is
whether we choose to accept it or not
It is not confined to, neither can be defined by
Your finite intellect, you just must accept and respect.

March 2 2007 3:43 PM

# Fabric of Reality

LIFE
IS BUT
A BREATH
OF GOD'S INSPIRATION
WHAT WILL WE DO
WITH GOD'S GIFT
BEFORE HE BREATHES IN?

# My Poetry

SHE IS MY POETRY
SHE MOVES MY EARTH FOR ME
MY EVERYTHING SHE IS TO ME
MY LIFE WITHOUT HER
EVER SLOWLY DRIFTS FROM ME
I NEED HER ESSENCE DESCENDING ON ME
LEAVING ME BREATHLESS
BUT GIVING BREATH AND LIFE AT THE SAME TIME
MOVING SWIFTLY TO LOSE MY MIND!!!
OH WHAT A SYMPHONY TWO BODIES MOVING WITH
SUCH HARMONY
EVER SOFTLY...
GENTLY...
STILL...
IS THE MOMENT THAT WE BECOME
ONE...
TOGETHER...
ONLY.

# PROVERBS

70

# My Proverb

REALIZED MY TRUE POSITION, CAUSE I WAS MISSING
SOMETHING THAT HAD THE POWER TO PROPEL ME
FORWARD
LORD
I AM LOST WITHOUT YOU
MISSING
LOOKING INTO A WELL FILLED WITH DARKNESS
I NEED YOU NOW
BEFORE I PERISH
PLEASE SEE ME THROUGH
CAUSE I CAN'T DISTINGUISH THE REAL FROM THE FAKE
I'M IN THE MIDST OF ENEMIES AND THEY SERVE ME A PLATE
BUT IT WAS ON THE TABLE YOU PREPARED SO I HAD TO SAY
GRACE
TO FACE WHAT COULD BE MY DEMISE
LORD HEAR MY CRY!
I'M DESPERATE

# Lucid Moments #4

My oh my, when will we learn that life is but a vapour, but a breath. What will we do with the time we got left. I have learned a lot over the past couple of weeks. We should learn to really let things roll off of our backs and not take things as seriously as we do.

We usually Major in the minor things and Minor in the Major things; we should turn this around.
Love without limits of your regular. Cherish every waking moment you have on this earth.

Love everybody you can to your fullest, in time they will do the same. You don't know the next time that you will see them or touch them alive.

FORGIVE, PEOPLE!!! it's not worth the stress. Stress is one of the number one killers of our human race, let it go!!!! GET OVER IT!!!! I'm sure you have done people wrong as well, ask for forgiveness and move on.

# The end?

How am I supposed to feel about this?
Sometimes I feel alone even when I'm with you
This is not supposed to be
Alone consumes me
To the bitter end
Silent words are so quiet, its deafening
Move me from this madness
I thought this was forever
But you deny me yourself
Is it what I know it is?
or what you tell me it is?
better yet, what you show me it is?
Cause I feel the change, like from fall's breeze to a winter's cold
It's strangely different from what I once dreamed it would be
But is this the final finale?
Does the buck stop here?
Is this the manifestation of all of my fears?
Captured in this moment
frozen with all our care?
Know you were the one but we are reduced to a tear
A fragment of what we were, pieces on the ground
We said our fighting words
now look where we are now
Is this the end?

# Blind Dark

It's harder than it's ever been
It's harder now ever to win
With you it should'a been easy
Now I feel you don't even see me
Clearly, things changed
Suddenly there's no shelter from the rain that are tears
Sweet to bitterness we've experienced throughout the years
Cares no longer matter
Suffocation to the end of us
No longer we trust
Hiding from our frigged cold touch
One another we no longer want
Blind eyes with cold stares
The hollows filled with fear
Everything seen in hinds site
No more ever clothed with light
Darkness became our hiding place
The dark to match our sight
Drowning to non-existence
Like being in murky deep water, our water becomes air
Intoxicating feeling but in reality it killed
The very fabric of us

# Lucid Moments #5

It's a crying shame, and now but a dream, that we'd will ever live till we are old and gray. Gone too soon is now the motto and punchline of our young today. We can kill someone and go to bed easily, wake up and eat breakfast as if nothing ever happened.

Humanity has absolutely no regard for life, only when it comes to our own. After all, it is all entertainment, right? I mean, we rap and sing and talk about killing people and harming them all day, like smashing in their face and ribs or blowing out one's brains. We cheer when we listen to it, but when it happens to someone close, it's not entertainment anymore.

The thing is, it should never be entertainment. This is real life! when people are gone, they ain't coming back. As much as one won't want loved ones gone before their time, don't take the life of another.

We should all strive for better.

# Lucid Moments #6

Don't worry they'll come. When the flashing lights start and others gather around to witness the magnitude of what you have accomplished, the naysayers, the haters will all come.

Family and friends alike will all see what they were supposed to see when they rejected you. And you will arise from the ash of bad words and say, "you should have believed when I told you it was to be true". Now behold God's plan, fulfilled destiny. I love the feeling of haters and naysayers under my feet. lol

# QUEEN

78

# Mirage

Today I saw someone that looked like you
And through their eyes, I felt you
Your loving too
Watching me to ignite the passion that once was again
Through her eyes I see you
Hoping that it'll be you
From afar too far for me to gaze at you
So I look at her to get a glimpse of you
Is it wrong?
cause you now gone
and its been so long since I held you
Strong
Only in my memories, do you live
Giving me the strength to take care of these kids
In whom I know, you living on through
I can't forget your love
It's like a familiar old fragrance
That when you smell it, it brings back memories racing
Man, it got a brother chasing.
I am your love

# Alive Now

I'm alive, and I feel so good
Doing all the things that I know I should
Are we just delaying the inevitable?
No longer feeling like a criminal
Freedom round the corner
Prison in my rearview
Major lights insight
You or your memories
Home court advantage
Think twice
Damage done
Confusions here but kicked to the curb
Honesty knocks again
Nobody's fool
New beginnings, fresh viewpoints
Two perspectives
Fork in the road
See you again or see you forever
Either way brighter days
Time moves slow but fast at the same time
Explain
Strings attached, games played
Mind chess, Mind checkers
No competition
Choices to be made
Choices made
War raged

# Queen's Touch

A king needing a queen's touch
Her power overwhelms him to charge him up
But yet she is not depleted
Together they cannot be defeated
She gains her strength by pleasing him
He battles all day just to please her
One in the same inseparable
Loves strongest bind keeps them together
This king only sees her and she makes sure of that
Others look but can't touch simple as that
Royalty shines through them
Queen so strong her lips are like a beacon, bringing him
home
Her thighs like a treasure trove, he wants nothing else
His mind is consumed by her and she makes sure of that
Like a helpless drone but still in control
Gives her the reins
She takes no advantage
No power struggle
She gives of herself willingly and freely
No strings attached but her heart

# Queen's Touch...

She knows the power she wields
But she must allow him to ravish her
Because he is King and she is Queen
And he needs her to survive
Like our bodies need the sun
They cannot stay apart for long without connecting
She is Queen and he is King
Her nectar he drinks daily
Power for the next day
It pacifies him
It is her pleasure to please him
He is her baby
Her general
Her love
Her king
And she makes sure of that

# Write, Right?

I'm in the mood to write
To write things right
To make things right
To make plain sights
Might fix my plight
Dawn turn nights
Quick like switch
Turn on lights
It hits me twice
It's easy believe me
It was my vice
Bloody murder
Bloody nose
Head leaned back
No control
Crack of whip
Lifting stacks
After stack
my back Snaps
Another dollar another day
Pressures of life stay
Pleasures of life wane
It all decays
Brighter days?
Hope so....

# Yearning

My soul yearns
My eye cries
My body screams
For the touch of you

My hair stands on end
don't have to pretend
you know me inside out
and outside in

when you are with me
I am alive
fill me ever still
from your fullness
bring life with you
when you come

I need every drop
cause on the daily it's
sapped from me
recharge me once
overflowing
utopia

# RUMINATION

86

# Moment of Truth

I only looked for the crumbs of time
that fell from your table
The little bit you had
When you were well able

Wish I had more to give
To make lives more stable
But I missed the mark
So my heart is in peril

It's my problem now
Always has been
You are not to blame
You are not responsible
For taking away my pain
Sorry for relying on you to make me be

They say if the shoe fits
Wear it
And your words are shoes because they bare your soul
So I wear it

Never meant to detract from you
Only to add
If I was insensitive I'd take it all back
But this road we go down is a winding one
Where we can't see the end or where we began
Unless the end is now and we are no longer friends

# Moment of Truth cont...

Things I wanted to avoid from the beginning
Loss of friendship
Loss of the bond between us that was so tight
So right

But I wear your words now
So I understand, right?
It will take more than pleasure in the bed to be a man

No Forgiveness Needed
Eyes were wide open when I was feenin
Now it will hurt all the more now
Cause our souls were cleaving

But to put things into perspective or back to normal
Things will have to become formal, again.

This is what happens when passion and pain collide
We become victims of emotional genocide

I apologize
It was supposed to be therapeutic for both of us
Never knew I was draining your very essence
I guess that says more about me
And less about you
Because I've become an addict to your time
Wanting more and more
Sometimes forgetting that you have responsibilities
Even though I try to give you as much space as possible
For YOU and I and Us

FORGIVE ME

# Passing Legacy

What Legacy will you leave on this earth?

Will people know your name?

Would they know that you stood for something greater than yourself?

Or would you be another statistic?

Create a name for yourself, and make it last throughout the generations.

Just A Facebook page with my name on it will not cut it.

The earth must quake and know that I was here.

While people move on and live their lives, you become a passing thought.

Will that be you?

Don't settle for less than what you know you are capable of.

I refuse to be another sucker, buried in shoulda, coulda, woulda.

What about you?

# Tears and Pain

Tears break ground
Splash, splash, no sound
Cringing gut-wrenching pain
No sufficient reasons
Love's containers shattered
Unexpected decisions pierce the soul
Choices made for future benefit
Lost in translation personal definitions
Disappointing roads taken
Brighter views ahead
Wishful thinking
oh that love might return again
Crazy cutting ties
No lies so no anchored madness
More difficult to swallow
Things must be done
Voids cant be filled with another
The end results will be won
But for now
Tears and pain

# Broken Reflection

Mirages of the past
Hourglass pass
No more holding time
Walking on shattered glass
Sand scattered round
Symbol of memories
Wind blows
House falls
no strength
Lose all
Anger all
Sorry!
Sorry excuse
For a human being
Sometimes fall
Might give way
Even if given all
Apologies
Not adequate
Can't heal all
Unseen wounds
A pact with pain
To give to get
Broken ties
Lives in regret

# Sanity's Insanity

This winding circle
It feels like enough
Looking up at light fixtures
Seems somewhat abrupt
The thoughts in my head
Turning corrupt
Hope
What is it
No longer caught up
A bribe to myself to keep it all up
Lost in a cue of questions
With no answers insight
I try and I try with all my might
Despair around the corner
Love turns a blind eye
Take my time to say my goodbyes
to sanity

# ADULATE

94

# Abandoned Stone

An abandoned stone, a disregarded Gem
That has been kept enclosed and thrown away by them
But picked up by me because I did see
The true worth of the stone or what it really could be
Locked away for months, true beauty cocooned
This gem was real... But, this gem was really bruised
its capturers were the ones that truly were fools
They did not choose to keep something
They felt would deplete in value
They had no codes, no picks, no keys
To crack open the safe, where this rare stone would be
But since I found the safe, I gave it all my attention
It whispered through the iron, I need your love and affection
Through these directions, we made a connection
And unlocked the safe without deception

# Perfect Gift

You are my perfect gift
My most truest friend
You are my arm in arm soul-dier
I'll love you till the end

You are my freshest breath
when I couldn't breathe at all
The most perfect scenery
when God finally made me see it all

You are my perfect gift, perfecting every day
Even with your imperfections
your very imperfections have become my perfecting tool
Cause when we're together, God uses us to perfect each other
A love so subtle

# Let's Make Poetry

Let's make poetry
to the sounds of the autumn air
Let's make poetry
to the sound of the birds and the bees over there
Kissing your air
softly
Speaking with our thoughts
Making sweet poetry
Locked

# Us

Thinking about you constantly
Your mind on mine forever be
Lost in your world you lost in mine
Don't need to turn back the hands of time
Cause we are here in the moment
We took it so we own it
Nothing stopping us
No pretending
Our eyes are open
We collecting
The love that is due us
We give it to us
We satisfied
They see right through us
If love is blind then we'll blindly do us
No turning tides
Love
The ties that bind

My love has grown and that's for sure
Letting go of my past has freed me up to love
And so much more
You inspire me to be a better man
With God and you, I know its possible
Your love I feel
It's tangible
Like the air, I feel
It's incredible
Possibilities are now endless with you
We can conquer anything
Mountains are see-through
I'll do anything to be with you
We have been through many things to get here
Ups and downs ins and outs
Scared was my motto
But that perfect love casts out all fear
So it's gone
Waiting to see what the future holds
So we can hold our future
Very strong
We face it together we are bold
I am very happy now
You make me very happy
I'll make you very happy
I honestly think I have found my soul's mate
In you
My heart
It beats for you

I'm so in love with you...

# Inspired

# Contagious

Contagious
Yes
Is your smile
I've been waiting...
Yes
For a while
Your company
I'll cherish to keep
I'll honour
To the souls of your feet
My heart
Was so undone
But with you
I shall overcome
Our journey
Has truly begun
We'll rise
Just like the sun
We'll take our time, that's for
sure
Your hurts
I'll not ignore
Our hearts
Will be intertwined
Our Body, Souls, and Minds.

# Our Special Gift

We loved you even before we knew you
Before the colour of eyes
the shape of lips
the touch of hands
To softness of kiss
We loved you
Way before we knew

You visited our dreams
to stir hopes to flight
To spend a day during the darkest of nights
A boy, a girl
Taking turns to sight
We loved you

My baby, our baby
new life begins
new hope wins
Legacy's choice reigns down
God's promise fulfilled
We won't peek behind the veil
On your day he will reveal
Everything we feel, all in all
Perfect detail
Our Special gift

# QUESTIONS

102

Why don't you expect men to look at you the way they do?

I mean, what did you expect?

I mean, you look good!

When you're dressed like that don't you think that you would look all the more appealing?

Let's be real!

So why be vexed when men look at you?

Cause obviously you dressing like that for attention, right?

Or is it that the ones that you are not interested in are the ones that are looking at you?

If "fine" is what you feel you are, should you feel offended or bothered by a look?

Is it that you want to be admired by all, to just some?

Maybe you're lying to yourself, maybe you're dealing with affectation.

Maybe you feel ugly inside and you need others to validate you.

Maybe you don't know the real definition of true beauty.

Sorry that I've also fallen victim to your insecurity, masquerading as sex appeal and self-confidence.

Why should I feel less than small because I misinterpreted what I felt was self-confidence?

Masks are all I see, should I even want to know you?

Maybe you are too broken.

Too much baggage.

Just because I see you with beauty, those are just my eyes

and since they're just my eyes, that's a very small scale in the grand scheme of things.

If I were the only one that saw you were beautiful and it was true, then that would be as "fine" as you would be.

But if you were not, and I still saw you as such, that would be on me because it was my eyes that were the beholder, the beholder was me.

So I'll end this encounter with just a gaze hoping that you are what you portray.

Beautiful

# Beautiful Questions

# Missed Communication

Silence is the way that we speak now
Unload the backchat with the cut eyes
Hoping one another would read between the lines
But it's hopeless, we're hopeless
We only see what we wanna see
Forget vocalizing
We only wanna be what we wanna be
At each other's throats
Till someone bleeds
Is the way we communicate now
It doesn't have to be, but it is and I digress
And we could try to see
Through the pain we caused each other to be
It speaks volumes to the cores of who we are
Will we ignore the pleas of our soul's cry
Or continue to cause each other to die
Shadowy voices in the background
Say, "he ain't gon change"
"She'll remain the same"
I wonder if they know, they only add to the pain
This chasm gets larger
Because we're being ripped from each other
What once was one to the fibre, becomes two through fights,
tooth and nail
Looking for an opportunity to bail
When it rains, it hails

# Broken 2.0

Broken
I'm
Broken
You're
Broken
I
Broke
You
I broke it
but I broke two
So I broke me too
While I broke you
I broke me
Ripped us
to the core see
Ripped us to the core me
Our core was true
I cored you
While I cored me
So I cored us
to the core see
dust

to the core be
Our core sees true
trust can no more be
To us can no more see
Core us to the core be
Just to the core us two
No care
No fear
I dared
to destroy us too
Rage to flame
A bonfire
Blew
Cannot be tamed
us two

# The WAKE Up Call

WAKE UP!!! WAKE UP!!! WAKE UP!!!
I hear the rattling of dead men's bones,
It's such a high pitched tone
That if I hear it I know it reached the throne
Of God
Nothings in'em, empty nothing in'em
Sucked dry by the things of life
where's the witness or the voices crying in the wilderness
All I hear are dry bones rattling
it's sad to say that the state of the church is baffling
If I see, I know Christ sees, believe it, and he's not pleased by what he sees
His bride to be is in a comatose state, asleep
Can't move, won't move
Spirit and the bride say come, but Christ says wait!
She's not ready yet, she's full of spots and blemishes
Looking for signs and experience
But when she opens her mouth all I hear are dry bones clamouring

WAKE UP!!! WAKE UP!!! All ye spiritually dead
Not a bride ye have become but dry bones instead
Religion has gripped you sin has bit you
Barren she has become, fruit she don't bare
The walking dead, she walks around as if she don't care
God looks in her and says where is the fear? Of Christ?
Wake up!!! And walk to the light, to become a light, to be like Christ
Come back to your first love, stop being ashamed of me
If you continue in your sin you shall become my enemy
Just remember he loves you, just remember he cares
And if you trust in him your burdens he will bear
Come back to life, come back to me
WAKE UP!!! WAKE UP!!! WAKE UP!!!

# Who Am I?!

Who am I?

Am I who they say I am?

On this journey to finding me, I've met with a lot of pitfalls, a lot of setbacks, and many wrong choices I've made.

So many things I'd not abstained from.

I've cheated myself many times from receiving the fullness of the gifts God has for me, because of my selfishness.

Who am I? I ask it again.

I feel like I've been running from my true self by running from God I've been running from my truest self.

On this road to finding myself, went back on my word many times, and I disobeyed God's word many times.

I should be more upset about not keeping God's word than mine, but I guess my pride gets in the way. Where I am worried about what people think about me keeping my own word rather than me keeping God's word.

Hypocrisy!!!!

I feel like I am suffocating, and can't find my way out.

I feel hopeless.

I've tried and I've tried, but nothing seems to work, but have I really tried?!

AAAHHH - Scream out loud, nothing but temporary relief.

How to set my soul free from the bonds of sin, my soul cries.

Where's my inspiration to sing, write, live, laugh, and love?

Where am I?

How do I find myself, to be set free, to breathe again? Help me breathe again.

Who am I?

So, I'm a beast now?
guess I've always been
according to you
I'm always him
Guess I'm beast now
Visceral
No empathy
Just don't care
Start off calm
Response be swift
Maybe stern
But you mistake me for him
When I deny, you insist
I resist
You see me as such
I become
Thoughts manifest
Misrecognize me for him and him for me
Are we one in the same?
Indistinguishable?
Guess I've never been me
Ever been me
You ever me see?
memories forgotten
Carnage of beast
Release

BEAST Mode
BEAST Mode
BEAST Mode
BEAST Mode
BEAST Mode
BEAST Mode
BEAST Mode
BEAST Mode
BEAST Mode
BEAST Mode
BEAST Mode
BEAST Mode
BEAST Mode
BEAST Mode
BEAST Mode
BEAST Mode
BEAST Mode

# ELEGY

110

Dedicated to my first queen
Oliesa Providence John
My Mother Forever
August 27, 1958
-
February 1st, 2022
God's Handmaiden
Daughter of zion

# True Heart

Momma, this has truly been one of the hardest times in my life. Our family lost our pillar, lost our ROCK. I am still in disbelief, this just doesn't feel real. Uncharted territory, discussing burial plots, headstones, legacy, caskets. This is not something we ever thought we'd be facing right now, but I am, we are.

Each condolence is a nail into hope's coffin, giving birth to a reality without you. Unreal.
All I wanted to do was Honor you my first Queen and lay you to rest, sending you home to our Lord in the best way possible. You were the best of us!

The best mother your sons and daughters could ever have, best Auntie, the best friend, amazing wife married over 42 years. The most loving Grandmother and sister. You lived to see most of your prayers fulfilled Momma! You will never be forgotten, your memories will be kept in my core's depth. I wish I could love you to life, but for now, l love you forever, still, always.

# SUPER

I thought my mom would live forever
To be Adorned in the finest of gold and most expensive silver
She was superman, wrapped in superwoman
She was Superhuman, my superhero
Invincible
She was my everything
Her superpower was her super faith
A woman of maximum faith
Faith's full expression
Put on full display without delay
She would never hesitate to back up her desires with scripture
Kindness and selflessness embodied her
Grace, she wore it around her neck like fine jewelry
And sipped from the cup of humility like fine wine
She touched so many lives
Witnessed too many she came in contact with
With the gentleness of her voice, she calmed storms
Encapsulated words as advice to reverse the curse or plight
She was the realist of the real
Would never talk bad about anybody
Always there to uplift
She was my mother
The best mother, wife, friend

# Where Are My Tears?

Where are my tears?
I don't know
Somewhere between
I can't remember and did I ever know to cry
I mean, I know I'm supposed to cry
I'm supposed to be in a ball curled up
Broken in half then broken again
Broken inside, broken in pieces
Broken in mind
But yet, no tears in sight
Where are my tears that I need to cry for my mother
The one held to hug her
The ones to tell her that I love her
I'm in anguish, with no tears for relief
Ball in throat
No release

Pain increased
Tears deceased
Kidnapped by disbelief
Held hostage by all this grief
Choked up on the inside, my tear ducts can't breathe
It's like I want to be broken, but I can't be
I got to keep strong, so they can't see
In a real way, man I can't speak
In a real way, man I can't see
No tears here to flush me
Feel like a dam holding my tears back so I can't sleep
Can't find the dam to break free
Pressure building up, so I can't be
They say we all handle loss differently
So I may be holding them somewhere
My tears for tomorrow
So that I can shower them on your memories Momma
Just to ease the sorrow
Where are my tears?

# Suddenly

Memorialized in my heart's chest
Your love
Never laid to rest
Your song's voice, ever softly serenade my memories
Arise sweet aromas of your essence
They flow to my childhood
Flow back to adulthood
I wish they could resurrect you to life, to be with us
Once More again
Momma, this pain is beyond the realm of the real
Truest feelings concealed
Have to be strong
Big gap missing
My rocks gone
How do we carry on without you here
Toughest choices must be made
Too much, not enough
Plague
All of a sudden suddenly proclaimed
Wind knocked out, never reclaimed.

# Till We Meet

I wish that I could scream
Scream so loud
That it could break through the very fabric of what separates us
Spirit and body
Rip through the Veil
For you to hear that I love you
Again
The unimaginable happened
Now I can't hold you
Only your memories can be held by my mind
But it is not enough
I want that touch
That physical touch
Our grasps
To hugs
Forever long to not let go
Forever us
Our Eve's Adam why did you consume that such
Putting key to door
Locked out
Miss you so much
Death is the door
Grave is the key
Wait on the other side
There waits my heart should be
Long tears cry aloud
My arms do sleep
Outstretched
My soul
Till we meet

# SHORT STORIES

120

# I Felt Your Love

I JUST FELT YOUR LOVE
SOMEWHERE THROUGH THE COSMOS
I JUST FELT YOUR LOVE
IT TRAVELLED OVER DISTANCES
OVER MOUNTAINS OVER VALLEYS
IT CAME DOWN TO THE MUCK AND MIRE TO FIND ME

I FELT OUR FUTURE  COMFORT ME
IT WAS AMAZING
I SAW OUR FAMILY
OUR BABIES
I SAW OUR HOUSE
 I SAW MY SIDE AND YOUR SIDE ALL ABOUT

THE CRAZY THING ABOUT IT IS
I DON'T THINK I'VE MET YOU YET
BUT OUR ESSENCE DID CONNECT

I FELT THE PURENESS OF YOUR LOVE WRAP AROUND
ME
AND IT WAS HEAVEN SENT
IT BREACHED MY HELL TO FIND ME
IT WAS REALER THAN ANY PHYSICAL REALITY
OUR SOULS WEPT AT THE UNION

I HAVE BEEN WAITING FOR THIS MOMENT
AND IT SEEMED LIKE FOREVER
THIS WINTER HAS BEEN THE COLDEST IT'S EVER BEEN
EVER
WITHOUT YOU

# I Felt Your Love Cont...

I KNOW YOU HAVE BEEN WAITING FOR THAT MAN
THAT SPECIAL ONE
BUT I WAS NOT READY YET
I WAS BEING PERFECTED THROUGH FIRES
HAD ONE FALSE START
LEARNT THE MANY THINGS THAT COULD TEAR US
APART

BUT I'M BETTER NOW
WISER
IF I HAD GOTTEN YOU WHEN I WANTED YOU
I WOULD HAVE DESTROYED YOU AND US WITH MY
UNRESTRAINED LUST
HOPEFULLY, I WILL NOW GET YOU WHEN I NEED YOU,
WITH US BOTH ABLE TO TRUST

BEFORE THE SANDS LEAVE THE TOP PART OF THE
HOURGLASS
TIME HAS PASSED
YOU HAVE BEEN PATIENTLY WAITING FOR ME
YOU HAD YOUR OWN BATTLES AND SCARS
NOW I BELIEVE GOD IS SENDING ME
I'VE DONE MY DIRT AND DID MANY A WRONG
TOLD MANY LIES AND CAUSED MANY A SCAR
BUT THROUGH THE PROCESS I HAVE BECOME A HEALER
OF THEM ALL
WHAT I USED TO DESTROY, I NOW RESTORE

# I Felt Your Love Cont...

I FELT YOUR PRAYERS TO GOD
ASKING, WHERE IS HE?
WHAT IS TAKING SO LONG?
WHAT COULD IT REALLY BE?
BUT A DAY IS AS A THOUSAND AND A THOUSAND AS A
DAY
YOU HAD TO BECOME
AND I HAD TO BECOME
WHAT GOD NEEDED US TO BE
WE HAD BECOME

YOUR HEART IS PURE AND I FELT IT
I FELT IT FROM MY GENESIS
IT'S LIKE WE WERE SEPARATED BEFORE WE GOT HERE IN
FLESH
AND WE ARE TRYING TO FIND OUR WAY BACK
OUR SOULS WILL NOT BE THE SAME UNTIL THEY
RECONNECT

# I Felt Your Love Cont...

THERE ARENT ANY NO'S IN YOUR VOCAB FOR ME
ONLY IF IT WOULD RUIN MY DESTINY
LOVING, KIND-HEARTED, HUMBLE PEACEFUL,
CREATIVE, SPONTANEOUS, AFFECTIONATE,
SELFLESS, NON JUDGEMENTAL,
ARE JUST A FEW WORDS TO DESCRIBE YOU
ALL OF YOUR ATTRIBUTES CAUSE BEAUTY
WHICH DRAWS ME TO LOVE YOU
YOU ARE SWEETNESS TO THE FULLEST
THERE IS NOTHING I WON'T DO FOR YOU
KEEP IN MIND I'VE NEVER MET YOU
BUT I FELT YOUR LOVE
A VIRTUOUS WOMAN IS REALLY HARD TO FIND BUT YET
I FOUND YOU
THERE ARE MANY WOMEN BUT OUR GOD LET ME FEEL
THE WIFE IN YOU
I FELT YOUR LOVE

# Endless Love

I see us living on the second floor of a house in the Plateau. The house has white exposed brick on the inside of our home. We have two large plants, one next to the window with a beautiful view of the mountain and one in our bedroom near the window. It's a small plant, a little scraggly, but we are giving it a lot of love and attention, he will grow really strong one day.

Our bedroom isn't too large, but it's just right for us. We have an old record player which sits on our large vintage wall unit with a large collection of jazz vinyl records that we play almost every night. We sip on wine while we dance, enjoying our very essence. We are so happy and full of love. In those moments everything is forgotten, everything is small. Our problems fade away and become insignificant.

Your lightly sprayed perfume lights up my mind evoking memories of our younger selves, a younger time. We are married now, and I think about how our love has blossomed over time. It has matured into something grand, something to inspire others on clear display. We have a cute white cat; she is so fluffy and loving- she fits right into our family.

It's winter now but we are warm inside. We are expecting our firstborn baby girl. I saw her in my dreams last night, so precious, she had your eyes, your lips, my smile, she was ours, our little creation. Our love could no longer be contained, it had to be expressed in human life. I rub your feet and your tummy every night. I lay my head on your tummy to hear our baby's heartbeat, it is loud, and it is strong, it beats in unison with yours and mine.
She will be an athlete one day, a runner, 100m,200m dash, and hurdles, we cheer her on in the stands. I see her running very fast, she breaks records in all that she does.

# Endless Love...

She flourishes In school, she is so smart, she takes after you in school, there's nothing she can't do, she is amazing just like you.

It's spring now you're a lot bigger, our daughter stretches inside of you at the sound of her daddy's voice, big stretches now. She wants to come out and join in our love on the outside, but she has a ways to go.

The end of summer is here, there's been a lot of rain as of late, they say the blessings are in the showers. We are on the way to the hospital, it's very warm outside, the drizzle from the rain gently kisses our faces, they gently dance upon our hands as if in agreement with our Union and in anticipation of our creation. The rain dances, the wind blows, the sky smiles with the rays of the sun, all wanting to see her. You smile, you smile at me, and gently touch my face as if to say, what you've always wanted is here, our prized possession is almost here only to strengthen the bond between us, to solidify the bond. Labour was major pain but it was also poetry, you brought forth with such magnificence, something beautiful, heaven-sent.

She is 2yrs old now, she got the cutest dimples because she has been kissed by God. She has the softest hair, wants to do everything by herself, so independent already. She has the chubbiest legs, I just want to bite them up. She has the most contagious laugh; it makes everyone around her happy. Her Grandmas love her to bits. She sits on Grandpa John's lap he holds her tight.

It's bedtime, I sing her sweet lullabies, there are no tears in her eyes, no fear in her skies... She is so aware, so intelligent, she knows what time it is. She loves her Mommy and Daddy. This is Our love our endless love.

# Where Were We?

I remember, there was a time when you would visit me in Toronto and actually shed tears when you left me. I felt that energy, even as I sit here while you are asleep, I feel our past and it taunts me. Our past haunts me, it taunts me, those tears of you missing me. You missed me even while you were with me and missed me while we were away from each other.

Those memories haunt me because they seem so far away they seem so far from present reality, the ghost of what was and not what is, haunts me. So many fond memories, times of travel, times of escape, so hopeful. We were able to laugh with each other, be ourselves with each other but things have changed now.

Where are we?

Over the years we've become jaded, both having disdain for each other, on some level in one way or another. Animosity, resentment, dislike, and hate are the undercurrent under the rug, just waiting to be punctured by an argument or a disagreement. Waiting to shed light on the past hurts, irrespective of the relevance. It took me some time to realize that our love is gone. Glimmers of a crumbled present, reminded of a glowing past, reflections off the shattered glass, we are broken. Seems like beyond repair, looking past the façade, the hurt is there. Broken.
I like the way we are able to be civil despite our blowups, but we need to face what happened, after all that was said and done, we are broken.

I was told there was a funeral, with no one in attendance but you. You never told me about it, was never left any clues. So I questioned you about it, tell me bout the girl I once knew.

Where is She?

# Where Were We?...

You said she is dead and gone, don't ever bring her up again, lost forever is her touch.

DON'T LIE TO ME!

Where is she? that bright-eyed girl, that lit up when she saw me, travelled miles to see me, where is she?

That brown skin girl, that put myself before her

Where is she?

She is dead and the warmth of her smile has faded, cold to the touch. Do you know the one that could melt fridged cold hearts?

Where is she buried? may I pay my respects?
She is buried deep inside, by the house under the deck, and you killed her!
How?
Over the years you drained her of life, she became the sacrifice to your selfish ambition, anger and rage, never to revive again.

Hopefully, true love could resurrect her, I need to resurrect her.

Is it too late?

# THE RIDE

I know that there's no communication between us
But you showed up in my dreams last night
I know you wanted us incommunicado
But you approached me last night
In my dreams, on a bus
We danced like strangers do
Separate
With eyes only
Desperate
To talk to you
To hear your voice


We were on a moving bus but the bus wasn't moving
You whispered to a friend close by
There he is
There's that guy
This feeling was so strong I couldn't stop it
Couldn't suppress it
It drew me to write this
To release me from this weight
Pulling me to this state

On the bus
You had a lot to say
On how I hurt you
You were in pain
How I hurt you at the beginning of our relationship
With the unforgettable
These things still haunt me
To my core, they haunt me
In my dreams, you made it clear what I've done
To haunt me

# .THE RIDE..

Victim and perpetrator
The actions of the undeveloped young
Mind of the dumb
With a loaded gun
Full
Frustration and lust all in one
Crazy ammunition
To the very...
Done
On the bus you were angry, telling me a lot of truths, I couldn't get a word in
Pain from the roots
You came off with a jacket bigger than you
What was I to do?

I had to chase you
Round a block
Into a building
To say
That I'm sorry
From beginning
To end
To tell you that my thinking has been thinking about you
Apologize for the pain
For not hanging on
For giving up
Not carrying on
But you disappeared
Didn't know which direction you'd run
Dream shifts
Story done

# THE RIDE....

You filled my dreams last night
Lately, real world and dreamworld have been merging.
So what's real and what's not have been blurring
Emotions and things have been stirring
By the sandman I know he's been lurking
Sprinkle pain with memories
Disturbing
The peace
Decreased
Oh I'm certain
A release
Now deceased
Draw the curtains

I'm not looking for things to change
Not even looking for a reply to this
thing
I just wanna say
That I must say
I'm sorry.
Help me to let go of this pain
Let go of these stains
Chained to the past no longer a game
Pressure cannot be contained
Hard to maintain
Two to blame

# End Here

This journey of mine, none with to compare
Has left me vulnerable, open Soul too bare
I hope you can glean from emotion's release
Lessons I've learned to garner some peace
I tried to be honest with the feels that I've felt
Mastered this art with the cards I've been dealt.
I hope you gain clarity or at least entertained
Till next time, no words that remain

# Connect With the Author

https://www.instagram.com/kingchozen1

https://www.linkedin.com/in/kaleeljohn/

Printed in Great Britain
by Amazon

38149782R00076